Celebrating the Master's Christmas

100 Years of Joyous Christmas Memories

Celebrating the Master's Christmas

100 Years of Joyous Christmas Memories

Writings by
May Harris Gray

Paintings by
Charles Peer

New Leaf Press

First Printing: September 1996

ISBN 0-89221-328-0
Library of Congress Catalog: 96-69683

Unless otherwise noted, all Scripture quotations are from the New King James Version of the Bible.

Dedications

To Jean and Louis Peer,
Tom and Rita Gray
– May Harris Gray

To my parents and grandparents for establishing our family Christmas traditions and to my girls, Cecilia and Jordan, for helping make wonderful Christmas memories.
– Charles Peer

With Appreciation

I wish to express my appreciation to the editors who have granted permission to reprint certain articles, including Charles N. Boehms, of Georgetown College, Georgetown, Kentucky.

– to the staff at New Leaf Press for assistance, and family and friends for their encouragement.

– May Harris Gray

With great appreciation to the owners of these paintings:

"Second Sight" - Dr. & Mrs. Michel Muylaert
"Colors in the Snow" - Dr. and Mrs. Jan Wubbena
"Winter Coat" - Dr. and Mrs. LeVon Balzer

– Charles Peer

Paintings

Introduction

In my hundredth year, the love of family has grown even sweeter. So now, my publisher has asked that I put pen to paper and record my memories of Christmas over the last century, to fashion a sequel to **Tending the Master's Garden***, a book collaboration with my grandson, Charles Peer.*

From oil lamps to my touch-lights; from carriage rides to my Globus tour of Europe by Air France; from an early explorer walking by a river without a name to a man walking on the moon; from my school writing slate and chalk to the computer that typed these words: I am confident that even greater things will be accomplished in the coming century.

My hundredth Christmas Day has dawned bright and fair. I am still called "Mama Gay," the affectionate name a grandchild used because he could not pronounce the letter "R." Warm in memory are the many traditions of the Holy Day, even now; candles glowing, the camera focused and the album still open, as we call out the old familar phrase . . . **Merry Christmas and a Happy New Year!**

A heartfelt "Thank You" from the publisher to May Harris Gray, Charles Peer and their families for sharing their family photos, and special memorabilia in these pages. You have helped add a special warmth and charm to these beautiful words and magnificent paintings.

Going back in time, one of my
earliest memories of Christmas is waking on a snowy morning
a little before the break of day in a fairyland world.

At the time I was born, the children in the family
did not see the Christmas tree until Christmas morning.

The parlor doors, which had been closed all of
Christmas Eve, were open. There stood a beautiful tree decorated with long strands
of popcorn, silver and gold foil, and candles. But the best part of this surprise was
a cuddly rag doll, and in my stocking – candy, two apples, and an orange. Good
news must be shared. I awakened Mama and Papa from a soundless sleep and joy-
fully showed them the gifts that Santa left for me.

Christmas
Morning

Earlier than usual the kerosene lamps were shining brightly,
for the wicks had been trimmed and the globes polished.

My belief in Santa Claus was firmly established
from that far-off day to the present, so you see,
the spirit of Christmas is still alive
in the hearts of children of all ages.

When about three years old, I rode with my father and our doctor in a carriage (with-the-fringe-on-top), as we made our way to the Christmas celebration at our church.

My first embarrassment as a "public speaker" took place at the church . . . I had been asked to "recite" a Christmas poem.

My Sunday school teacher who taught me my verse sat at a desk facing the rows of seats in which the audience was sitting. I practiced and practiced always facing her with my back to the audience. No one told me to do otherwise, so that night I came out in my new white dress, turned to where the desk had always been and recited my speech – my back to the audience. I wondered why everyone laughed.

Santa Claus (he was fat then, too) kindly turned me around to face the audience and ask me to say my "speech" again.

Strangely enough, Santa's voice sounded just like the voice of our doctor.

(To give you some perspective on the time-period, William McKinley was our 25th president. Occasionally, such television programs as "A&E" carry grainy black-and-white "moving" pictures of McKinley; this will give you an idea just how far May Harris Gray has come!)

Getting Ready for Christmas

When snow on the frozen meadow is lying,
When trees are bare, the sky overcast . . .
When the wind in the chimney is crying, crying,
It is then I remember the past.

Then too, we were getting ready for Christmas,
Hearing the Story, tying a bow.
Our stockings were hung on the mantelpiece –
Three stockings in a row.
I longed to be tall. My arms could not reach
Above the first bough of the glittering tree;
Longed to be grown as those who seemed
Ten feet above me.

The wish has come true.
I am hanging the garlands
That link the chain of our lives.
The bells are ringing – the old year is dying;
The yule log is burning, the stockings are hung,
(Three stockings in a row)
And the wind in the chimney is crying.

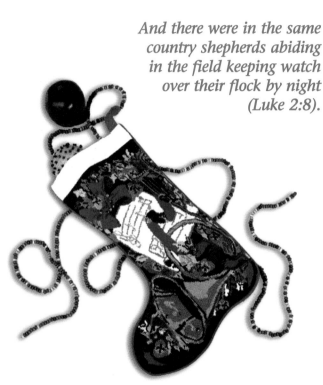

And there were in the same
country shepherds abiding
in the field keeping watch
over their flock by night
(Luke 2:8).

A Child's Dream

Verily I say unto you, Who soever shall not receive the kingdom of God as a little child, he shall not enter therein (Mark 10:15).

He heard the sheep bells tinkling low;
He saw the shepherds wondering go
To find the Child of Bethlehem.
All night he dreamed he followed them.

Followed as the star shone down
Like gold upon the hills around.
He knelt beside the infant King
And heard the choir of angels sing.

For him the bells will always ring
Who thinks he heard the angels sing.
For him the Christ is never far
Who thinks he saw the Christmas Star.

Miracle in the Snow

The celebration of the Christ Child's birth captures the imagination and reminds us of everything we hold dear.

At times, it is a mood or an impression that defies words that we remember instead of some great event.

When about eight years old, I was walking with my parents to our nearby home after the Christmas Eve church service. I was sure a miracle was taking place. The bright moonlight on the falling snow created an air of expectancy. My parents, and the enchanted little one between them, are still in my mind . . . reminiscent of Victorian days gone by.

Christmas carols and tinkling bells floated up and down the streets. Lamps were shining through the windows of the homes and the real meaning of Christmas possessed me and filled my heart with joy. There was no need for words as we walked along. I was so happy, hand-in-hand with Mama and Papa; how I loved them!

Always the Stars

We may not remember
Our Father's grace
When the noonday sun
Is high,

But always the stars
Proclaim His love
Against a darker sky.

When we spent Christmas at my grandmother's home in Kentucky, never once did I dread the oncoming night. I looked forward to it.

About twilight time, the horses on this tobacco farm were watered at a large stream not far from the house. Though small, I was allowed to ride one of the ponies. Of course the water was icy-cold, but in the summertime we waded in the cool stream.

After dark I enjoyed sitting near the large fireplace – helping, as best I could, to shell corn from the cob and watch it being popped over the coals in a long-handled "popper" made of wire.

Then I was finally tucked in a trundle bed for a long night's sleep. These low beds were on rollers and stayed under the high-bed during the day. Bed-steps were placed by the high-bed – two heavy wooden ones. Both these and the corn poppers can be seen today in antique shops.

It has been said that something of the child remains within us.
I believe this maxim to be true. Although quieter, I still enjoy evenings.
Visiting with friends, reading, writing, or painting is always
relaxing. And always I can recall the breath from
the nostrils of that pony from
Christmas so long ago.

Note to a Brother

*Your old men shall dream
dreams, your young men shall
see visions (Joel 2:28).*

Do you remember the frozen river
And cutter's row on row,
And how our ponies pranced to the rhythm
Of sleigh bells in the snow?
Like something made of magic
I heard the Christmas bells today
And listened with a joyous heart
To the music far away.

I lean to see the sleighs,
But only the fiery strike
Of pony hoofs on stone
Sparkle in the night.
Only the sound of bells
Drifting across the park,
And one by one the stars
Waiting for the dark.

For whom are the ponies prancing,
And where could they have gone?
Why does the sound of bells
Ring for me all night long?
Across the drift of years
When many a tale was told
Could we be dreaming still
On the way to growing old?

The Broken Sled

More than a phantom scene, these memories are as vivid as sunshine and the shadows.

As superintendent of a life insurance company, my father was transferred from Kentucky to northern Illinois.

At my new school, after the opening prayer by the teacher, the pupils were allowed to select the song of the day. I raised my hand and stated my selection. Not being accustomed to my southern drawl, I suppose, those in the room were unusually still, which bothered me not at all. The thing that bothered me was that no one knew my choice of songs, "My Old Kentucky Home." Nor did they know my second choice, "Swanee River." When I announced my third choice, "Old Black Joe," the room burst out in laughter.

I remember experiencing a very lonesome feeling. No one knew my songs and no one knew my name.

Because I would turn in my assignments at school in verse form, my classmates would ask me to write their invitations for Christmas parties. This gave me some popularity. Despite the unknown songs and my broken Christmas sled caused by mischievous boys hiding stove-wood under the deep snow, I loved my school and my cold winters in the north.

While Christmas bells rang out and Christmas songs were sung, we baptized one another in what seemed to be mile-high drifts of snow.

During the fast-moving sleigh rides, heavy lap robes wrapped tightly around us kept out the biting cold. When the mercury was very low, heated bricks wrapped in the robe kept our feet warm.

A little before bedtime, we gathered around the organ and sang our favorite Christmas hymns. My mother played the old organ quite well. Nearer than the falling snow, nearer than my hands and feet, was the warmth of my heart.

The last day of school before the Christmas holidays, after the opening prayer, Christmas songs were sung before we rushed home to games, celebrations, and gifts.

As my two sisters and I grew older, we recognized the exceptional ability of our parents to instill an air of reverence throughout the day.

In many of the Christian families, the father read the age-old story of the coming of our Redeemer before the Christmas gifts were opened. Thus, the true meaning of Christmas was never secondary.

These enduring observations remind me of family and friends I knew so long and loved so well.

Rondeau Redouble for Christmas

When Christmas comes and the air is carved and still
Summer birds have flown to warmer lands.
Where rain trees rained their gold on an autumn hill
We hold the treasure in our open hands.

Here where a road runs by the sun-bright sands
The children come, and even the smallest fill
Their arms with winterberry and ivy strands
When Christmas comes and the air is carved and still.

Men drag the great yule log across the sill –
And see? In the reaching light a trimmed tree stands
As if it had a mission to fulfill . . .
Summer birds have flown to warmer lands.

Imbued with the music of the spheres that spans
The stars, the branches speak of peace goodwill
Toward men as snowflakes fall like swaddling bands
Where raintrees rained their gold on an autumn hill.

This is the season of hope, of doubts that chill
And sear the mind. Only the Word withstands
To glorify and some small faith instill.
We hold the treasure in our open hands.

So lowly a place, how great the great God's plans.
So small a Child, how high a star to distill
Such luminance the wise man understands
What warmth the Word, all holy, can refill
                          Our hearts when Christmas comes.

*In the beginning was the Word, and the Word
was with God, and the Word was God. The
same was in the beginning with God. All things
were made by Him; and without Him was not
any thing made that was made (John 1:1-3)*

The Horseless Carriage

The Christmas gift of one of the first automobiles was indeed a major happening. For young people this is especially difficult to understand, with all the styles and colors and sheer numbers of cars currently on the road. But then they were a novelty.

This Model T Ford had strong headlights, high seats, and no doors. Therefore, with the adults proudly occupying the seats, my best friend and I sat on the doorless floor, our feet on the running boards.

These reflections almost cause me to lose track of time. In returning mentally to those early days of newly discovered gas lighting, unlocked doors, and indoor plumbing, all things seemed possible.

Many other automobiles followed this first Model T in our town.

Drivers were cautious. Horses were afraid of these horseless carriages and often bolted or ran away with their helpless passengers. However, these two modes of travel were soon compatible and motoring was a perpetual delight, especially when the town was adorned with enchantment of Christmastime.

The First Christmas

Our years are numbered from that first Christmas Day when the God of heaven and earth gave the world its greatest gift, His only begotten Son.

This child of promise, this child of Immaculate Conception came, not in the robes of a king; not in a mansion befitting a king. His attire was the simple swaddling clothes of the period. His bed a manger of straw in a crude stable in the small town of Bethlehem in Judea.

The Saviour of Mankind came in love to a desolate world whose people were praying and waiting for the fulfillment of the prophecy that a Messiah would come.

As the heavenly angel announced the unity of the finite with the infinite, the star that stood above the birthplace of our Lord glowed with a radiance that spread far and wide.

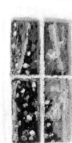

Like the wise men and the shepherds, we, too, can walk in the light of God's love as we seek, find, and bow down in the holy hush of prayer.

The Open Door

On this eve of the Christ Child's birth
Let us open wide the door –
It opens from within . . .
Somewhere on the lonely road
A wanderer in the dark of night
May ask to enter in.

Let the songs of praise ring out,
Let the organ music roll
Until the very rafters move.
Somewhere in the crowded street
A stranger, lost, will surely need
The reaching hand of love.

Open wide the door this night
As if the Christ Child stood without
His entrance to implore.
As the starlight wraps us round
He will enter . . . He will come
Through the open door.

*Behold, I stand at the
door, and knock: if any
man hear my voice, and
open the door I will come
in to him, and will sup
with him and he with Me
(Rev. 3:20).*

Despite the fascination with autos, the more tried-and-true methods of transportation continued to dominate us for a time.

My sisters and I often played with dolls in the family buggy. This is not to be confused with the jet-set accessories available for today's Barbie Dolls!

One day, due to our carelessness in leaving our Christmas dolls and their clothes in the buggy in the carriage house on the alley, they were stolen. We were brokenhearted and the promise of new dolls hardly consoled us.

Teaching a child right from wrong was truly exemplified that day and something good came out of the experience.

Late in the afternoon, a poorly dressed woman knocked on our back door. With her was a little girl with a small wagon. The wagon held all that had been taken from our carriage house.

"I don't teach my child to steal," said the woman.

My mother kindly assured her that she had demonstrated that fact, and that she admired her as she embraced the tearful child. Thoughtfully, my father asked if we had a doll we could do without. We did, and hastened to place it with its small trunk of clothes in the wagon along with oranges, apples, and candy.

Tears became smiles as the little girl and her mother turned toward their home.

And suddenly there was with the angel a multitude of the heavenly host praising God, and saying, Glory to God in the highest, and on earth peace, good will toward men (Luke 2:13-14).

To those who heard these words that first Christmas night, how far off peace must have seemed. For years they had lived under Rome's military might, persecution, and jealous, oppressive rulers.

Even though not yet attained, we know the promise of our God will be fulfilled, even as the promise of a Redeemer was fulfilled; peace between nations, peace between heaven and earth, peace in the heart.

Although God's real world is holy and eternal, He is concerned with earthly situations and the answer for problems in our lives. We cannot touch God without being changed ourselves.

Remembrance

The two of us, so busy all day long,
Stood at dusk and looked upon the land
So lately green and intimate with song.
A star's soft radiance brushed my open hand
Softer than wings and still as a child's
      still sleep –

And we remembered,
Sharp on the edge of tears that high bright star –
The faith of the shepherds deep as the sea;
A mother's hopes and fears.

It is as if the angels, too, recalled
And placed this silver star high and bright
To light again a shining path for all
Who seek the Way this Holy Christmas night.
We know the world has changed, but not its need
For the God of peace and love, of Word and deed.

Let the words of my mouth, and the meditations of my heart, be acceptable in thy sight, O Lord, my strength, and my redeemer (Ps. 19:14).

Interrupted by War

My teaching career began in Louisiana when I was 17, but I soon moved to the beautiful and historic city of Fort Smith, Arkansas. Fort Smith, for those who appreciate history, was the home of Judge Isaac Parker during the last century. He was known for swift justice in his court, which was always full of outlaws and various desperadoes. But for so many lovely years now, the city has settled into its role as a friendly link between the past and present.

During World War I, my future husband, Tom, was stationed at Camp Martin in New Orleans, LA. This made for a somewhat sober Christmas holiday during December 1917. Our boys were fighting in places whose names most Americans couldn't pronounce. We busied ourselves, trying to provide some comfort for those "over there," as the slogan went. I remember in particular knitting scarves for soldiers. The ladies who labored at these gifts received much satisfaction from this, for we knew winter war was particularly harsh in France. I must confess, however, that a scarf I knitted surely had to be worn by a very tall soldier!

The war ended during the Thanksgiving season, 1918, and we eagerly anticipated the arrivals from Europe. So many were sick upon their return, for a terrible influenza epidemic had broken out, even in America.

Christmas is a day of fact and faith, of poetry and song: a day of praise to the God of love for the gift of His Son, the Son who bore our transgressions according to the mercy and will of God.

It has been centuries since the shepherds and Wise Men knelt in reverent devotion before the Holy Baby of Bethlehem. And yet from that historic time to the present each generation has been aware of the need for Christian motherhood.

Although the virgin Mary, the mother of our Lord, was bewildered as she listened with awe while the heavenly messenger announced that she had been chosen by God to be the mother of the Christ Child, with spiritual awareness this saintly young girl voiced praises:

> *My soul doth magnify the Lord, and my spirit hath rejoiced in God my Savior (Luke 1:46).*

During these years of grace, this godly mother has been looked upon as the ideal model to follow as mothers point little eyes to the stars, and little souls to God.

Because He Came

We gathered the bayberry in the lane –
Thorns pierced the frozen stem
And we remembered a longer road
That led to Bethlehem.

We broke the fragrant cedar and pine,
Gathered the cone and burr
Remembering prophetic gifts
Of frankincense and myrrh.

Oh, to have lived in the Holy Land
We would be reconciled;
We could have folded the lambs to rest
And knelt beside the Child.

If we search with heart and soul,
In some starlit kneeling place
We can find Him, we can share
His glory and His grace.

Search the scriptures for in them
ye think ye have eternal life: and
they are they which testify of Me
(John 5:39).

After my marriage in 1920, our Christmas celebrations were notable for the closeness of family ties. My sister-in-law and I made our fruitcakes together, gathered greenery with which to decorate our homes, and alternated the Christmas dinner from house to house, every other year. At this time our gifts were exchanged. Our son and two daughters were our greatest gifts. Of course, the festivities centered around them and my niece and nephew.

During my childhood, the emphasis for Christmas celebrations fell between December 25 and January 1, with a "calling-card day" eagerly anticipated by everyone.

This consisted of exquisite card trays that were set just inside the door of every home, usually on a small table. It was great fun to walk the neighborhood, your greeting cards in a case, and knock on doors.

Christmas was such a time for family in those days, that the only thing interrupting lavish celebrations was illness. Before vaccines, childhood diseases were rampant. The doctors reported these to the health department, which immediately placed a very large card on the front of the house warning people to stay away. They did, even to passing by on the other side of the street.

Jesus Christ was not born according to the natural laws of life.

> *Now the birth of Jesus Christ was on this wise:*
> *When as His mother Mary was espoused to Joseph,*
> *before they came together, she was found with child*
> *of the Holy Ghost (Matt. 1:18).*

The ageless story of this miraculous birth of the King of kings has been told over and over again down through the centuries. It has been, and is, an inspiration for the world's greatest artists, musicians, writers, and all others with artistic talents, and the blessed hope of believers everywhere, past and present. All have been moved by Christ's mission – establishing on earth the kingdom of love, peace, and saving grace.

As God enlightens us with His truth in the Scriptures, He reveals the power of the Holy Spirit to enrich the spiritual experience that assures us of Christ's redeeming love.

Christmas in Our Town

As once the light of a great high star
Fell with a golden radiance down
On Bethlehem and the hills around,
So shall I place a lesser light
On every windowsill tonight.
Light travels fast and travels far.

One lamp to shine on the crowded street
Flamboyant in the semi-dark;
One lamp to face the shadowy park,
And one to place on the kitchen sill
Slanting its light on the ice-blue hill
Children smoothed with velvet feet.

But listen and look: Like a trembling bell
From every street in our town
A song rings out, a light shines down
To lighten footsteps quick or slack,
Or help a stranger, lost, turn back.
It is Christmas again and all is well.

*Let the people praise thee O
God; let all the people praise
thee (Ps. 67:3).*

One of our most treasured Christmas gifts was our first electric refrigerator. This white, two-door Westinghouse with a round monitor on the top was beautiful. It made all the ice cubes we needed.

A Westinghouse Christmas

It was now no longer necessary to place the large cards in the front window notifying the iceman how many pounds of ice he was to put into the icebox. The blocks of frozen water were carried through the open back door and placed in the top compartment of the icebox in the kitchen. Through this same back door came the milkman to place our daily supply of milk in the icebox.

If one of my favorite memories is a much-appreciated convenience, my children have often told me that their favorite memory of Christmas Eve was lying awake until they heard the music played on the calliope as it made its annual visit up and down the streets of our hometown.

A prominent citizen in the community drove his large truck, in which a skilled musician played carols on the calliope. Since we lived only one block from the orphanage, we knew that we were assured of a longer visit, as it always stopped there for an extended period of time. Nothing can compare to the music that floated through the air on those cold, crisp, and very quiet Christmas Eves. This was truly a gift to our city, and one that was deeply appreciated.

Luxuries were quite hard to obtain for many people during the difficult years of the Depression and World War II.

Living through two world wars and the after-effects of the stock market crash have heightened my perception that there is no way in which we can prevent sorrow from entering our lives.

During the Depression, the Boston Store, a department store in downtown Fort Smith, added a grocery section on the third floor. This image stands out in my mind, especially of those lean holidays for so many people; it was a reminder, as I watched neighbors emerge from the Boston Store with groceries instead of expensive gifts, that our material blessings are not under our own power.

Candles, so a part of Christmas celebrations, were very scarce during the war years. The funeral homes could get them, but no one else.

Our thoughts, prayers, and gifts at Christmas, and all through the year, were for our soldiers, and during the Depression, for the homeless.

An Aged Shepherd Looks Back

And an angel said unto them, Fear not: for behold, I bring you good tidings of great joy, which shall be to all people (Luke 2:10).

On these fields
Where David grazed the sheep
And filled the air with such sweet music,
The light came down.

No blaze had ever matched the blaze
Of that bright light.

And I, who followed the light's
Golden path,
Who knelt before the Christ Child;
Who stood upon a hill near Bethlehem
At the dawning of a changed new world,
Still know that blessed hope,
That keeps eternal joy where all
Is peace, all love.

Santa Dolls

In the 1950s, I remember that Christmas decorations became more ornate. Christmas trees were larger and visible for a longer period of time, and homes received more decorative touches.

During this time my two daughters each had three small sons. For their world of dreams and beliefs at Christmas, I fashioned a pair of two-foot Santa dolls. These dolls were so loved and hugged each Christmas that they became quite disheveled.

One Christmas I offered to restore their lost glory (this was approved by my youngest daughter's three sons).

But the three sons of my oldest daughter, who were younger, would not hear of it. They wanted Santa to stay the same as he was in their childhood.

The forty year old Santas, one like new and one in disarray still occupy their accustomed place on the fireside hearth, keeping watch.

In the area where I live, the term "White Christmas" has been a some-times welcome realization. The Ozark Mountains are lovely in winter, with snow dusting the hills. On occasion, we have had blankets of snow deposited in our area.

So the stage was set for a visit from my sister and her husband and their three sons.

They arrived for the holidays from their home in New Orleans. What was normal for our three children — snow — was a dramatic experience for the boys from the deep South.

After a heavy snow had fallen in the night, the shades were opened and my nephews were so stunned, there was complete silence until the youngest managed to shout, "SAND!"

To them, this world in white could only be compared to the familiar, gleaming white sands on the Gulf Coast.

The Many Roads To Bethlehem

All day I helped my father tend the sheep
From field to field, and on this Night of Nights,
Weary, lonely and small, I fell asleep.
Suddenly it seemed ten thousand lights
Converged into a glory-beaming ray.
I longed to follow the shepherds where it led –
But knowing a little lamb had gone astray
I stayed behind and searched for it instead.

I found the little lamb beside the manger,
Its thirst slaked, its wounded side healed.
Strange, how vivid the memory, but stranger
Still, the light that encompassed the shepherd's field
Led all our paths, in poor or lush green sod
Onward to the Child, the Lamb of God.

And it came to pass, as the angels were gone
away from them into heaven, the shepherds said
one to another, Let us now go even unto
Bethlehem, and see this thing which is come to
pass, which the Lord hath made known unto us
(Luke 2:15).

Dressing for Success

Another terrible war pushed its way into our lives in the 1960s. Vietnam touched us even in the idyllic setting of northwest Arkansas, where pumpkin patches and smoke-plumed chimneys are a world away from rice paddies and jungle.

These years of my life were spent delighting in the attention of my grandchildren, because the ever-increasing fabric of life is growth in our young people.

At Christmas, I did my best to directly affect the growth of my grandchildren.

They loved the turkey dressing that I made for Christmas and Thanksgiving each year. This *astonished* me, because I was not considered a gourmet cook!

The year that I decided to turn that responsibility over to younger hands brought such wails and complaints that I almost rescinded my order.

But I stood firm.

Although they were sure that they would not like their mother's dressing, and she wasn't sure either, they ate it. Guess what? They've been eating it ever since.

Pleasing impressions made in childhood are never lost, perhaps because of awed wonder and uncluttered minds. Even with the flawed natures we are born with, childhood innocence is a thing to be nurtured, so that we can carry some goodness into a world that demands alertness.

This has been a reminder to me every holiday season.

Occasionally, the family here spent Christmas with my youngest daughter and family who, at one time, lived in another city. We should all be grateful when family can gather at Christmas, and not worry about schedules and program conflicts. Ease of travel has become one of our precious gifts.

After greetings, naturally we admired the decorations, not the least of which was the beautiful crèche. These, for so many years, have come in a variety of styles and detail, but they can become such a family heirloom. It is always moving to sit and meditate on the nativity. Contentment and devotion are beyond measure. We pause before the crèche as we focus our thoughts on the deep meaning of this Holy Day.

It is interesting to note that the three sons, now with homes of their own, searched and found a crèche just like the one that was so dear to them in childhood.

He Is Come

Be still, troubled heart,
At ease, doubts and fears,
Gabriel hails a virgin
And Mary hears.

Be calm, wind and wave,
This, the sacred birth
Will change the warring world,
Be silent earth.

Christ the Lord is come
His blessings we entreat –
And lay our gifts of love
At His feet.

And thou shalt have joy and gladness; and many shall rejoice at His birth (Luke 1:14).

The Flocked Tree

Christmas celebrates the gift of God's only Son. This gift is from the hand of God to His children.

Christmas through the years has brought a decided increase in elaborate decorations and festivities, both in and on the homes and main streets and avenues. During the energy crunch of the 1970s, all outdoor decorations were discouraged.

A regrettable trend: in many places the display of Christmas symbols are not allowed. Never did I expect this to happen.

Twenty years ago or so, the popularity of "flocked" Christmas trees, using a white substance we could spray on the tree, caused me to go back in my memory to those early years.

With heavy "lap robes" wrapped around us, we scanned the woods for that perfect tree, found it and brought it home. We stood it firmly in a bucket filled with a few heavy rocks, sand, and water. We then decorated the tree with paper chains made of crepe paper, strings of popcorn, and candles. In later years, we bought trees cut from tree farms and sold by organizations and decorated them with store-bought ornaments.

You can see how a "flocked" tree would run pictures of dozens of past Christmas trees through my mind! Now, of course, artificial trees are available in green or white.

Fruitcakes that were once an important part of the Christmas menu are seldom made in the homes now. The cakes were made before Thanksgiving many years ago, so that they would have time to "season" and were given as appreciated gifts to friends. Often, as was our custom, families joined together for the annual baking ritual.

These are the things that lingered with me as I entered my "retirement years."

Bells, Starlight, and Song

I will never hear a Christmas song,
Never hear the joyous ring
Of bells but I shall want to bring,
Though gone these many years and long,
All of the loved ones home.
        Whenever I see a star burning
Like a flame in the Christmas sky
I turn toward childhood and the dawn
Of other Christmas days – lest
The blazing fires of late December
Grow cold and I no more remember
Eager footsteps by the door.

I never see a yule log glowing
When night comes down without knowing
Hearts will soon be going, going
The homing way once more.

*Yet setteth he the poor on high
from affliction and maketh
their families like a flock
(Ps. 107:41).*

The Swift Feet of Time

Now I've seen a hundred winter seasons. Like "The Old Clock on the Stair" by Longfellow, our clock's pendulum swings steadily back and forth from year to year.

The past ten Christmases, I have stayed in my own apartment in my son's home. I owe a deep-felt gratitude to family and friends who brighten the day with greetings and gifts.

Rewards come in many ways. The air throbs with excitement as we view the smiling dolls that fill the branches of the "doll tree" in the parlor, and gather around the stately tree in the family room, glistening with ornaments and garlands of light.

The recording of past and present events requires a retentive memory. It seems only yesterday that, after the death of my husband, I spent each Christmas Eve with my oldest daughter and family who live near. While they attended the Christmas gatherings of her husband's family, I kept busy wrapping some of their gifts and listening, really listening, to the angelic Christmas anthems on my favorite TV channel.

Reliving certain events is often a rewarding experience. My youngest daughter's home comes to mind.

Not to do things by halves, her husband added to his train collection each Christmas. The many tracks circled around and around the Christmas tree. The little trains, like living, breathing organisms, delighted adults and children alike, as they whistled past each other, switched tracks, or stopped at the lighted depot.

Christ, A Spring of Living Water for All Who Thirst

Since the Saviour of all races was homeless, at times, many nations claim Him as their own. They picture Him in their own dress and color. He speaks and writes in their own tongue.

This all-inclusiveness enthrones in the heart and mind of all who follow in the footsteps of the Prince of Peace, joy beyond measure, faith, peace, and love.

Although the personal ministry of Christ our Lord ended centuries ago, His work, through His church is still carrying on His mission.

Even though at different times in history the burning fires of faith in the Lord of all have risen high or flickered low, they have never been quenched.

To all who stand thirsty by the well, our risen Lord still freely offers an overflowing cup of Living Water.

The Day From Which Our Years Are Numbered

We have seen His star in the east, and are come to worship Him (Matt. 2:2).

What of the glow in the eastern sky
Like a diamond mounted on heaven's floor?
What of this jewel silver-white?
We have never seen this star before.
What of its mothering embrace
Of a Child and a stable of mystery?

The earth is honored – this is the place
That shows the way of history
Revealing the birth of the haloed King.
On this bright path, fixed, unmoved,
Came earthly kings. We too, can bring
Ourselves and all that we have loved.

Altar In Judea

And with haste Aram, the faithful shepherd, left the manger and his worship of the tiny babe to carry the blessed tidings of the new-born Messiah to his beloved wife, Sibyl, and their own infant son . . . the two he loved best in all his small world. A world linked by night to his flocks upon the hillside pastures and by day to a tiny, rough-hewn cottage nestled under the whispering olive trees and the rustling palm.

Aram's quick footsteps awakened Sibyl from a dreamless sleep and for a moment his words had no meaning; then her slowly awakening consciousness heard him announce the arrival of their long-awaited Messiah . . . heard him say, as though addressing their own sleeping child.

"Little Lamb, in Bethlehem lies another babe, our Messiah. We will hasten there and, though I am not worthy that He should come under my roof, I shall beg of Joseph and the holy mother to bring Him and be our guests. You shall have the honor of sharing your bed with the infant Jesus; His touch shall make you blessed all the days of your life."

The last words were addressed to Sibyl and now an alert awareness was in her eyes; an assured certainty was in her movements as her eyes scanned the small bare room as though seeing it for the first time. To her, this home which had been her refuge and her world, suddenly seemed mean and small. Sibyl's hands fluttered to her trembling heart, and with pleading words her voice faltered.

"Aram, my beloved, what are you saying? You cannot bring the Messiah to our humble dwelling. Go back to the palace of the King with an offering and with prayers, but pray do not bring Him to our home.

It is so bare and small. Our linens are, of course, homespun; our bowls are molded from the poorest clay and our son is so young his cries would annoy the royal family. Do you not know, beloved, that our home is too humble to receive the Messiah and King?"

Aram sighed; a sigh so gentle and so blended with the fruitful olive bough against the sloping roof that it was imperceptible to Sibyl. A force as strong and intangible as the starlight shadows on the wall was in his voice as he answered, "Sibyl, Sibyl, do you not know? The King is a babe born of a virgin mother. There was no room in the inn and so the Holy Infant was born in a stable. He sleeps in swaddling clothes in a manger of hay. We have no gift to offer except the gift of our heart and of shelter. Come let us hasten that He may abide with us always. "

Aram was silenced by Sibyl's gesture of impatience. "Aram, what are you saying? No people would allow their king to lie in a lowly manger filled with hay. Do not tell me He is the Messiah. I saw no star and heard no songs in the night. No welcome awaits a child born of a virgin mother and whose only bed is a manger of hay."

"But Sibyl, we have ministered to many a stranger with our scant. . . ." Aram was suddenly silenced as he looked into his wife's eyes and saw her unbelief. Turning abruptly, he walked slowly to the door where his wife was standing and together they looked out upon the deep silence of the night that seemed to echo and re-echo their turbulent thoughts.

"Come with me . . ." and upon Sibyl's refusal Aram crossed the silent threshold of his door and went out into the night toward the little town of Bethlehem alone.

Sibyl had known fear, pain, and disappointment, but never a parting like this and few had been so swift yet so complete. She knelt beneath the Mezuzah which was fastened firmly to the door and spoke aloud in accents of prayer. "It is the first time I have failed to follow wherever his steps have led. What strange delusion was this that called him from his watch? Ah, Most High, blot from his memory this weird mockery, this strange defenseless dream. The promised Messiah will come some day. He is near at hand and His banner will be placed on the highest hill and every knee shall bow to the King of kings and the Lord of lords."

At last she arose, and later, lying across the bed, watched the stars grow dim as the glow across the horizon brought its promised day. But it failed to bring a glow to Sibyl's heart; she was conscious of two things only; Aram had gone his way alone and peace had gone out of her life.

As the moments passed she thought upon the mystery of what might be called the two worlds in Jerusalem, and all the lesser towns about. The world of those strange ones who worshiped many gods and could take their gods with them wherever they should go, and her own people who worshiped one God and whose only temple stood proudly in Jerusalem. Now . . . would there be another world all in this small land? The world of the shepherds and the Magi, and all those who even now were worshiping a tiny babe, born of a virgin mother in a lowly stable in Bethlehem?

As Aram left his own doorway and walked toward Bethlehem his troubled thoughts kept step with his steady tread. How now would he find peace in the home his hands had made if faith did not abide there also? His footsteps faltered, and as though in a dream, the shepherd turned from the narrow streets of Bethlehem and sought the hill-place where he tended his flock and where the great light shone from the heavens.

As he came upon the narrow path that led to the fast-rising slope of the hill, the old familiar way brought an element of peace to his heart. Below lay the little town like a shining citadel, and all about radiated the light of a star that hung clear and bright in the midnight sky . . . once more he was listening to the golden voice of the angel saying, "Fear not, for behold I bring you good tidings of great joy which shall be to all people." Again he seemed to hear the angel host singing, "Glory to God in the highest, and on earth, peace, good will toward man."

Aram's belief in the young Christ Child was steadfast now and constant as the Star of the East resting over the place where the infant Jesus was sleeping, and in the light of the star that looked down over the Judean hill he made a covenant with his God.

"On this hill I shall build my altar; his shining star shall be my guide; these dewy grasses my pillow of rest. The miracle of the Christ Child shall live eternally in my heart and shall be shared by my son who will come to know and be glad, as I am glad, that the Messiah was born in an humble palace: a stable clean and pure where innocents are given life and the food to sustain it. Thus, His followers will be sustained by these things which He has permitted us to see. So, in the sweet night brilliant with stars, the shepherd laid stone upon unhewn stone until his altar was as high as it was wide. He built it facing the sunset on the eastern slope of the highest hill of his own green pastures. As the fitful red glow of morning broke, Aram completed his joyful task and knew once more a deep and abiding peace.

After days of worship and watching his flock, Aram prepared to return to his beloved wife and son. Surely by now Sibyl would have gone to bow at the feet of

their Messiah; surely by now she would have perceived that His earthly kingdom was the invisible kingdom of the heart.

But harken . . . what of these rumors among the shepherds? What of a king whose name is Herod? What of the safety of the little Messiah and his own first-born? Once more the shepherd hastened to Joseph and Mary and the babe . . . this time to give warning of impending danger . . . then to his own home to flee with his wife and babe.

A dull, relentless fear crept into Sibyl's heart when the shepherd did not return from his watches at break of day. Desperately she tried to recapture a sense of peace, for many were the days that the shepherd had been compelled to stay with the sheep both day and night. Sibyl was obsessed with the thought that Aram was protecting them from some unknown calamity.

Her nights were troubled with uneasy dreams and now the day seemed to have come to which her sleepless nights had been leading.

As the gray twilight closed down about the little cottage, the tightening around Sibyl's heart was more than she could bear. Only half aware of what she was doing, the mother cradled the sleeping babe to her heart and crossed the darkening threshold of the door. She was going to find Aram and ask him to take her with him to a manger in Bethlehem.

The Shepherd's wife had not gone far until she knew some great disturbing force was over the land. Not one, not two, but many mothers were hurrying past carrying babes close to their breasts . . . had all the shepherds failed to return from their watches? What sinister shadow lay hovering over these Judean hills? In some manner the little town of Bethlehem had been darkly drawn to danger.

With a swift gesture of her hand, Sibyl attempted to hail a friend who hurried past, but cold terror was in the fleeing woman's eyes as she said without pausing, "Hasten Sibyl, the soldiers! King Herod has ordered his men to slaughter the babes of Bethlehem two years old and under."

Sibyl's dark eyes were enormous and pain-sharpened as she listened breathlessly to the half-finished sentence; the truth of the words seared the night, her mind, her heart. Now she remembered, Aram had spoken of Herod's fear of losing his throne to a king who had been born in Bethlehem and of his threat to do away with the babe. But she had turned a deaf ear to his every mention of the New Messiah, too late . . . too late . . . far and wide this nameless fear spread from Bethlehem throughout the country of Judea, and terror fell on the hearts of all.

The silence of the plains was broken and in the gloom of fading light soldiers marched upon Bethlehem and away from it, into the very pastures of the sheep ground. As the population spread, the shapeless fugitives took to the hills and plains under the nameless stars, fighting death and the fear of death. Behind paths and before, the soldiers stalked sullenly. Dark blots upon the ground and in rustic cottages bespoke the red blade plowing swiftly through quivering flesh. Even the dimness of the starlight failed to erase the scars of the night and the cries of terror penetrated the air, even to the very brown of the hills. A flashing spear, a reddened blade . . . then a silence more terrible than tumult.

Sibyl's feet were swift now, and the arms that held her first-born were her strength, for the lowering night offered no mantle of protection.

The shadow of danger, more fierce than pain, hovered over her and night merged into a darker night than she had ever known. Already, to her, it had been longer than the years she had lived, wider than the sky, more endless than time. Sibyl prayed to the God she knew, the God who promised His people that He would send them a Deliverer, "God Most High, Aram knew the Deliverer had come, and for his sake spare this babe and I will follow trackless paths around the world until I find this Messiah and worship at His feet."

It was past the midnight hour and still the dark mask of horror had not been removed from the land. Time and again she saw the mark of reckless cruelty and slaughter that shot its curse from Bethlehem to the sweeping plains and beyond. With fear shaking her like swift pain, Sibyl hurried through the highland wilderness toward Aram's pasture.

The shadows of night enwrapped all distant places and only the starlight overhead made a pathway before her. The steep grade of the hill was difficult to climb, but the mother did not falter. Now, a glance at the level ground told her she had reached that part of Aram's pasture ground that lay on the crest of the hill. As suddenly, in the track that lay ahead, a dark figure emerged and gazed into the valley below.

Silently, almost without breathing, Sibyl fell to her knees behind a cloister of stone that screened her from the watchful eyes of the soldier; as the same anguished and believing prayer arose to her lips, she had faith now in the coming of the Messiah, the deliverance brought to Israel. A babe who was found by following, with faith, the silver fingers of a star.

The soldier stirred. Closer now, and still closer he came, past the wide spreading fig, past the green and silvery foliage of the olive, and, after an endless eternity, as her heart scarcely beat, past the wide pillar of stone.

As the echo of the soldier's heavy tread died away it seemed to Sibyl that nothing could happen to this sleeping babe, so alive, so lovable, so peaceful. Hope came to her heart and a voice seemed to say, "You may go where you will." She wrapped the babe in her mantle and laid him tenderly upon the soft grass whispering as she looked about.

"Someone has made an altar of these unhewn stones. This surely is heaven's high temple opened above me. The Messiah has come. The glory of waiting Israel has passed by and made himself known."

Sibyl lifted a flat stone from the ground and placed it upon top of the altar-stone that an unknown hand had set in place, saying, "Behind this altar screen the fires of my doubting, burned out as this babe was spared to be a living witness for the newborn Messiah. The innocent babes who were slaughtered this night are His first witnesses, the first martyrs for the Saviour who is also innocent of the evils of this world."

The mother's words were like an incantation as she dedicated her first-born son to the Lord. As the purple mists of morning were rising from the plains she prepared to return to her home and renew her search for Aram; to tell him that his faith in a star had not been in vain, for she had also found the Messiah as she knelt behind an altar on a star-lit hill.

Soon Sibyl could see their tiny cottage gleaming in the early morning light. The cottage that had arisen out of the strength of their love. The cottage that would now afford a haven for the homeless Christ. The cottage that would stand as a monument of love and faith through the fullness of all their coming days.

But, who was this running as the hunted of the hills? Aram! Ragged and stained and torn, his face was bleeding from the thorn of the wilderness and his feet were pierced by the jagged rocks of the hill-country. Aram, the quiet, the gentle, now with terror on his face and hatred in his eyes, lips moving, calling the name of his son.

The incredulity in Aram's eyes faded to comprehension as Sibyl's trembling lips told him of the terror of the night and their refuge behind an altar of stone, told of her prayers and faith. "And now, beloved, let us hasten to Joseph and Mary that we may worship the new King and take them into our home as our guests."

Aram replied gently, "They are gone. When I heard the rumors I went first to tell them to take the babe away but they had been warned already. Then I hurried home, but you had also departed. So I searched for you all night long. I should have known to go first to my altar! I am not worthy of so great a blessing."

"Your altar?" And the shepherd's wife fell to weeping. "You are most worthy of all the shepherds: the first to find the Messiah, the first to accept Him and the first to go to Him and warn them of this night of tribulation, and He has bestowed upon you the gift of your son at His altar. I am the unworthy one. He has departed, and I cannot go to Him."

"But Sibyl, your faith was greater than mine. You accepted Him, though you never saw Him, and He will abide with you always. But we must remember always that the gift of this star was not for us alone. Just as it laid its silver benediction on our hearts, it will make men whole, as long as time shall last. Israel will pass through the sorrow and tribulation we have known tonight."

"In generations to come other rulers will rise up who will be jealous of our God. Again and again, nations will be thrown into chaos, their sons destroyed because these unbelievers leveled His temples in order to rule, for their little day, over a ruthless kingdom of their own."

"We who have been permitted to witness the coming of the Prince of Peace will pass the story of His coming from generation unto generation. In the dark hours of history men will take to their hearts, even as you did, all they hold dear. Over dark pathways, through blood and pain and tears they will keep their course straight and their faith true. As men look up they will find their star and it will lead them to their altar, to their God, and to peace."

The shepherd fell silent again and reverently they walked arm in arm to an altar each had made alone and together rededicated it in thanksgiving and in prayer; and lifting their eyes heavenward, they found an abiding peace under their own silver star.

All Praise

If I had watched with the shepherds there,
Been blinded by that high bright star,
I wonder if step by eager step
I, too, would have hastened to find the Child.
Or would my steps have slackened and turned –
Seeing no mansion for a King,
Fearing the skies would darken again,
Knowing the way was far.

All praise to those first worshipers.
Though awed by the miracle of light,
Bewildered by the heavenly voice –
Remembering some blessed hope
The shepherds knelt beside the child
And kneeling heard forever after
The heartbeat of divinity,
God's gift that holy night.

*Heaven and earth shall pass away but
my word, shall not pass away
(Matt. 24:35).*

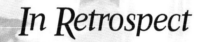

In Retrospect

*Train up a child in the
way he should go: and
when he is old, he will
not depart from it
(Prov. 22:6).*

Whenever I hear the Christmas bells,
See a star's pure light on snow,
I turn to childhood days again –
It is a path I know.

It leads to a chapel shining bright
In all its Christmas glory
As we pause to hear once more
The world's sweetest story.

It spans the years and leads where love,
In starlight all the way
Has kept the pathway bright from Christmas
Day to Christmas Day.

May Harris Gray received her education in Kentucky, Illinois, Louisiana, and Arkansas. A graduate of business college, she taught school and music in Louisiana before her marriage to Thomas V. Gray (now deceased) of Arkansas. Two daughters and a son blessed this marriage.

It was written of Mrs. Gray's literary skills, "Few Kentucky-born poets have received more recognition than May Gray, now a resident of Fort Smith, Arkansas. Awards totaling more than 130 include the Dylan Thomas award – Poetry Society of America, first place in the Book Award from the National League of American Pen Women, two John Gould Fletcher Awards, the Edsel Ford Memorial Award, and the Merit Award – Poets' Roundtable of Arkansas . . . to mention a few."
– Kentucky In American Letters, Vol. III

Her poetry has been published in many periodicals throughout the United States, England, and Belgium.

May Gray is the author of eight books. She is included in Marquis Who's Who of American Women, Who's Who of the South and Southwest, Who's Who in Arkansas, Midwest Poets, and Dictionary of International Biography – England.

Charles E. Peer grew up in Van Buren, Arkansas, where he received his first formal art training at the age of 12. He received a bachelor's degree from Hendrix College in Conway, Arkansas, and began graduate studies at the University of Denver, Colorado. Mr. Peer received his Master of Fine Arts degree from the University of Arkansas in Fayetteville, Arkansas, in 1979.

Mr. Peer established his studio/gallery in the Historic District of Van Buren, Arkansas, in 1980. In 1990 he and his family relocated to Siloam Springs, Arkansas, where he heads the Department of Art and Design at John Brown University.

Along with his teaching responsibilities, Mr. Peer continues to display his work in one-man and group exhibits and to lead workshops throughout the region. Mr. Peer's paintings, which have received recognition in many exhibits and competitions, are currently represented in several galleries across Arkansas, found in many corporate and private collections, and been used as illustrations by DaySpring Greeting Cards of Siloam Springs, Arkansas.

Charles and his wife, Cecilia, have been married since 1984 and have one daughter, Jordan.

Tending the Master's Garden,

the first collaboration between May Harris Gray and her grandson Charles Peer, is available from New Leaf Press.

The breathtaking collection of 32 paintings of God's glorious gardens, scenery, and landscapes bring the word-pictures of the acclaimed poet to life. Enjoy a walk through some of the most rapturous scenery anyone's ever seen. This collection of original paintings and poetry make *Tending the Master's Garden* the ultimate gift for a friend or loved one.

Visit your local bookstore and pick up your copy of this elegant gift book today for only **$14.95.**

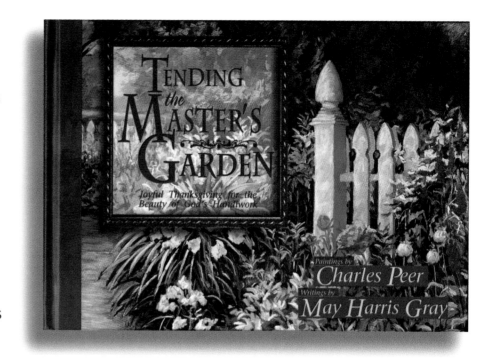

New Leaf Press........P.O. Box 726.......Green Forest, Arkansas........72638